Series Editor: Cath

D0524281

The **Faith in Action** Series

The Gangster Who Cried

The Story of Nicky Cruz

R. J. Owen

Illustrated by Brian Platt

RELIGIOUS AND MORAL EDUCATION PRESS

THE GANGSTER WHO CRIED

The Story of Nicky Cruz

One evening a boy wandered down a street in New York. Suddenly a gang of youths with leather jackets gathered round him. They knocked him down. One of them stood over him, flicking at his throat with a knife. Another punched him in the face. The boy's shirt was ripped off. He was held down as a huge 'M' was carved on his back with the knife.

As the boy on the ground screamed with pain, he was told: 'that'll teach you not to come into the Mau Maus' area.'

From the late 1950s through to the late 1960s the Mau Maus were one of the most feared gangs in New York. They had named themselves after a group of Africans who brought terror in Kenya before the country became independent. The gang went around the streets in black leather jackets with a red double M stitched on the back. They wore fancy hats, many of which were decorated with wooden matches. Most of them carried sticks. All of them wore sharp-pointed shoes. With these they could kick a man to death in a matter of seconds.

For over two years the leader of this gang was a boy called Nicky Cruz.

What Do You Think?

Important: in answering 'What Do You Think?' questions in this book, it is important that you not only state your opinion but also give as many reasons as possible for your opinion.

1. Why do some young people join gangs?

2. To what other groups can young people belong? Can these groups meet the same needs as gangs?

3. Why do you think gangs often adopt some kind of 'uniform'?

Life at Home

Nicky was born and brought up in Puerto Rico. This is an island in the West Indies and is part of the United States Commonwealth. Nicky was one of a large family. He had sixteen brothers and one sister. His parents were spiritualists. They claimed to have power over spirits, both good and evil. People paid them money to use this power to get in touch with the spirits of the dead. Often Nicky felt very frightened.

Nicky was unhappy at home. He did not get on with his parents. There was little chance of spending time with them alone. After all, there were eighteen children in the family. Besides, his parents were busy in the evenings with their work.

When Nicky was only five years old his father caught him taking money out of his mother's purse. His father was very angry. He locked Nicky up in a small dark shed full of pigeons. Nicky was screaming as the birds pecked at his face and neck. It was a terrible experience for a little boy.

One day Nicky's mother and several other spiritualists were sitting round a long table in the living-room. They were drinking coffee. Nicky came into the room. He was bouncing a small ball on the floor. He was now eight years old.

'Your Nicky's a cute boy,' one of the ladies said to Mrs Cruz. 'He looks just like you. I know you must be proud of him.'

The mother looked strange. She was staring hard at her son. She held her arms straight out in front of her. They were pointing at Nicky. She began to speak in an odd way.

'This ... not ... my ... son. He ... child of evil.'

Then she started to shriek at Nicky.

'Get out, Devil! Get away from me! Leave me, Devil! Away! Away! Away!'

Nicky ran to his room and threw himself on his bed. He was

very frightened. He cried. Did his mother not want him? Did nobody care?

The lack of love from his mother and father, and his fear of them, may explain why Nicky did so many wrong things. He stole. He started fights with younger and smaller children. One day he even hit a small girl on the head with a rock. While she was bleeding and screaming he stood laughing! He got an airgun to shoot birds. When he had killed them he cut their bodies into pieces. Indeed, Nicky was so unhappy that in his early teens he ran away from home six times. Each time he was brought back by the police. In the end his parents wrote to his married brother, Frank, asking him to look after Nicky. Frank agreed to do so.

What Do You Think?

1. Nicky ran away from home because he was unhappy. Is running away the only or best thing to do when a child or teenager is unhappy at home? Give reasons.

2. Is having a difficult home life a good reason for behaving cruelly? Why/why not?

Alone in New York

Nicky was fifteen when he went to live with Frank and his wife in New York. New York was quite different from Puerto Rico. It was crowded with people and traffic. There were also teenage gangs.

Within two weeks of arriving in New York Nicky had his first run-in with a gang. On his way home through a park he met a man who had with him a talking parrot. He was so interested in the bird that he did not notice that a gang of boys were forming a semicircle behind him. They were called the 'Bishops'. Nicky's talking and laughing stopped as the man suddenly walked away.

'Hey, kid, what you laughing at?' asked one of the boys behind him.

'I was laughing at that crazy bird,' replied Nicky as he pointed to the man with the parrot.

'You live around here?'

'I ... I live with my brother down the street,' Nicky stammered.

'Do you think, just because you live down the street, you can come into our park and laugh like a hyena? Huh? That what you think? Don't you know this is the Bishops' area? Man, we don't allow no strangers in our area. Especially those who laugh like hyenas.'

Before Nicky could answer, the lad pulled a knife out of his pocket. It had a seven-inch blade.

'You know what I'm gonna do? I'm gonna cut your throat and let you bleed like the animal you sound like.'

'Hey, m ... man,' muttered Nicky. 'What's wrong with you? How come you want to cut me?'

'Because I don't like your looks, that's why,' came the reply. The lad pointed the knife towards Nicky. He started to move towards him.

Another member of the gang spoke up. 'Aw, come on, Big Daddy, leave 'im be. This kid just got in from Puerto Rico. He don't even know what's goin' on.'

The lad with the knife hesitated.

'O.K.,' he sneered as he backed off, 'but one of these days he'll find out what's going on. And he better keep out of the Bishops' area.'

Nicky now knew that he

would have to be tough if he was to survive. He got into fights at school. He bought a switch-blade – a knife which springs open at the touch of a small button on the handle.

Nicky stayed with his brother Frank for only two months. He ran away after being expelled from school for hitting another pupil over the head with a chair. He was now on his own. To pay the rent for a room, he started to hold up people at knife-point and rob them.

One afternoon he decided to enjoy himself at a fun-fair which had come to the area. At the entrance gate he noticed a group of boys standing around. They were wearing black leather jackets with a red double M on the back.

Suddenly one of the boys looked in Nicky's direction. As Nicky came closer. the boys shouted out: 'Hey, baby, what you doing around here? This area belongs to the Mau Mau. We don't want no strangers hanging around here.'

The other boys with the black jackets gathered round, forming a circle.

'What gang you belong to, man?' asked the Mau Maus' leader.

'I don't belong to no gang,' Nicky replied. 'I came down here for the fun-fair. That a crime or something?'

The question was not answered.

'A square can get killed in a hurry. Maybe I kill you. Now, if you want to live, you better beat it.'

Nicky did not want to appear scared, but there were too many of them. So he nodded and slowly turned back down the street. He walked to a nearby park and sat down.

A boy of about thirteen joined him. 'Gave you a rough time, didn't they?'

'What d'yer mean?' Nicky muttered. 'I could have taken

ny one of them. But I didn't see no sense in fighting all of them
t once.'

'Man, these gangs are tough around here,' said the boy,
eaching into his shirt pocket and pulling out a home-made
igarette. He lit the cigarette. 'You smoke pot?'

Nicky shook his head.

'How'd yer like to try one? I got an extra. Man, it's cool.'

'Sure,' Nicky replied. 'Thanks.'

The 'pot' had a strange sweet taste and a strong smell. Nicky
egan to feel dizzy. Then he felt as if he were floating on a
loud. He gazed at his new friend.

'I thought this stuff was supposed to make you happy. How
ome you're not laughing?'

The boy of thirteen looked up. 'Man, what have I got to laugh
bout? My old man's a drunk. Only he's not really my old man.
He just moved in with my mother last year. And this man, he
eats up my ma all the time. Last week I tried to stop him and
he hit me in the face with a bottle and broke two of my teeth.
Then my ma threw me out of the house. Now I'm living in the
treets. What have I got to laugh about?'

What Do You Think?

1. Is expelling a badly behaved pupil from school the best course of action? Give reasons.

2. People who use illegal drugs often claim that they do so in order to make life more enjoyable. What problems could taking these drugs cause?

3. Some people have campaigned for cannabis ('pot') to be made a legal drug in this country, just like alcohol and cigarettes. Is this a good idea or a bad idea? Why?

Nicky Joins the Mau Maus

A few weeks later Nicky was invited to a party for teenagers. In
the dimly lit room, against a background of soft music, people
were dancing, drinking and taking drugs. Nicky stayed for a
while and was then taken to a side-room. Facing him was Carlos,
the leader of the Mau Maus.

'How old are you, Nicky?' asked Carlos.

'Sixteen,' replied Nicky.

'You know about fighting?'

'Sure.'

'You willing to fight anyone, even police?'

'Sure.'

'You ever stab anyone?'

'No,' answered Nicky honestly, but sadly.

'Two things, man. If you join the Mau Maus, it's for ever. No
one ever quits. Second, if you're caught by the cops and squeal, we'll get you. You have three days to think it over.'

Two nights later Nicky was at another party. Carlos greeted him.

'We have two ways to find out if you're chicken. Either you stand still while five of our toughest guys beat you up, or you stand still against a wall while a knife is thrown at you. If you run from either, we don't let you join the gang.' And Nicky knew that anyone who did not pass this test would be knifed, if not killed.

Nicky chose to be beaten up. He was punched and kicked until he passed out. When he came to he was bleeding, bruised and had a broken nose. Something solid was pressed into his hand. It was a revolver: Nicky was now a Mau Mau.

Within a few days of joining the gang Nicky took part in his first 'rumble'. A 'rumble' is a fight between rival gangs. This time the 'rumble' was against the Bishops.

The Mau Maus charged into a school playground. The Bishops were waiting for them. 'Kill 'em! Get 'em!' they shouted as they swarmed into the school-yard and ran across the open space that separated the two gangs.

After some hand-to-hand fighting the Bishops started to retreat. One of the Mau Maus yelled at Nicky, 'Shoot that one there! Shoot 'im!' He was pointing at a small boy who was trying to get away but had been hurt and was half running, half limping as he fell behind the fleeing Bishops.

Nicky aimed his gun at the staggering figure. He pulled the trigger. The boy kept running. Nicky shot again. The boy fell. He crawled a few yards. Then he lay still.

Suddenly the police arrived. Those Mau Maus and Bishops who could run, did so. But there were several who could not move – they were dead or badly injured. In a terrible way Nicky felt good. He had seen blood run. He had shot someone, maybe killed him.

On the way back, the gang's deputy leader put his arm round Nicky's shoulders. 'We're the same kind. Both of us are nuts!'

The next two years were filled with fights, robberies and gang activities. Nicky was so mean, so cruel, so tough, that when Carlos was arrested and sent to jail he was made the gang's deputy leader. Then, after only six months with the gang, he was chosen to be its leader.

Once, Nicky and six other

au Maus met a youth who belonged to a rival gang. Nicky knocked the boy to the ground and hit him with a piece of metal piping. Nicky kept smashing the piping across the lad's head and body until the youth had been knocked out and lay in a pool of blood.

Looking back at this and similar actions, Nicky now admits: 'I was an animal, without any sense of right and wrong.'

In fact, he was so bad that he scared himself! It was as if there was something evil inside him that made him do terrible things. He liked the sight of blood. He enjoyed hurting people. Yet deep down he felt lonely and afraid. He did not sleep well at night because of his fears. He had horrible nightmares. Often he woke up screaming.

He suffered in other ways too. In gang fights he was sometimes kicked and cut. Once he was hit over the eye with a piece of piping. The scar was there for a long time.

One day five boys from another gang came up behind him. They held him tight as they twisted a leather belt round his neck. He was almost strangled. After that he could not speak properly. There was always a funny noise in his throat as he talked.

Then the Mau Maus decided to make war on the police. There was no special reason for them to do so. It just seemed an exciting thing to do. Nicky wrote a letter to a police station and warned that any policeman who went into their area would be killed.

The police doubled their patrols. Often three would walk a beat together. The Mau Maus would gather on roof-tops and throw bricks, bottles and dustbins at the police. Sometimes they would shoot at them. They even threw petrol bombs at police cars and police stations.

To make war on the police was a stupid thing for the gang to do. The police were only doing their job. They were there to protect people from boys like Nicky. They were not going to stop because of threats or violence. Yet Nicky and his gang continued to attack them.

The way Nicky was living once led a psychiatrist to tell him, 'There's no hope for you. You're on a one-way street to prison, the electric chair and hell.'

By the age of eighteen Nicky had been arrested twenty-one times. Twelve times he had spent days in prison awaiting trial. He had been charged with almost every crime, from robbery to assault with intent to kill. He had stabbed at least sixteen people. Yet, in court, nobody would give evidence against him. Everyone was afraid that if they did, Nicky or his gang would kill them.

During the two years when he was gang leader seventeen people were killed by the Mau Maus.

What Do You Think?

1. Gang members had to undergo tests to prove their loyalty and courage. Can loyalty and courage really be proved through dares or violence? Give reasons.

2. Nicky thought that 'there was something evil inside him that made him do terrible things'. Could there be a force of evil either inside or outside a person which makes them 'do terrible things' or might there be other explanations for what is making them behave badly?

3. Why do some people regard the police as 'the enemy'?

'Go to Hell, Preacher'

It was a hot Friday afternoon in July 1958 and a few of his gang were wandering down the street when they saw about a hundred people gathered round a couple of men. One of the men was playing a trumpet. It was the tune to the hymn 'Onward! Christian Soldiers'. The other man was just standing still. He looked the skinniest and weakest fellow Nicky had ever seen. It seemed as if a puff of wind would have blown him over!

When the trumpet-player stopped, the skinny man climbed on to a piano-stool he had brought with him. He opened a black book. Then he bowed his head and prayed. At first the youths shouted and jeered. Then came quiet. Nicky felt strange. It was odd how everyone was now waiting for the man on the piano-stool to say or do something. Nicky was uneasy.

Suddenly the skinny man raised his head and, in a voice so faint you could hardly hear him, he began to read from the black book. It was a Bible.

'God loved the world so much that He gave His only Son, that everyone who has faith in Him may not die but have eternal life.' The man went on to explain how God loves everybody. 'God knows what you are. Yet he loves you right now. God loves you. You can be different! Your life can be changed!'

The skinny man was David Wilkerson, a 26-year-old Pentecostal church minister. Earlier that year he had read in a magazine about the start of a murder trial. Seven young members of a New York gang were accused of beating up and stabbing to death a disabled boy. As he read the report, a voice in his mind seemed to be saying, 'Go to New York and help them.' He believed this inner voice was from God.

David drove over 560 kilometres to New York but was not allowed to speak to any of the seven defendants. Instead, he tried to speak to the trial judge in the court but was thrown out by the courtroom guards and questioned by the police. As a result, his name and photograph appeared in newspapers and gained him a reputation for wanting to help gangs.

For several weeks David walked the streets and parks of New York, talking to gang members and drug addicts and later preaching at street-corners. This is what he was doing when Nicky met him.

When David finished speaking, he walked over to Nicky and stuck out his hand. 'My name's David Wilkerson. I'm a preacher from Pennsylvania.'

Nicky ignored the outstretched hand. He puffed away at a cigarette, shooting little jets of smoke out of the side of his mouth. Then he stared hard at David. 'Go to hell, preacher.'

'You don't like me, but I feel different about you. I'm concerned about you. I've come to tell you that Jesus loves you.'

No one loves me, Nicky thought, no one ever has. He remembered what his mother had said to him when he was eight – 'I don't love you.' Well, thought Nicky, if your own mother doesn't love you, then nobody does. This man must be a liar.

'You come near me, preacher, and I'll kill you!' he blurted out.

'You could do that,' replied David. 'You could cut me into a thousand pieces and lay them out in the street and every piece would love you.'

Nicky went off with his friends. They went to his

forgive them, for they do not know what they are doing"'.

Nicky yelled at him and cursed him. 'Get the hell out of here!'

'Before I leave, let me tell you just one thing. Jesus loves you.'

'Get out, you crazy priest! I'll give you twenty-four hours to get out of my area, or I'll kill you!'

David backed out of the door and smiled.

'Remember, Nicky, Jesus loves you.'

Nicky did not know what to make of it all. He felt confused. There was something special about this skinny preacher. There was something powerful about him. However, in front of his friends, Nicky acted tough. 'That stupid, crazy witch! If he comes back here, I'll set him on fire!'

What Do You Think?

1. What possible explanations might there be for the 'voice in his mind' that David Wilkerson heard?

2. Why do you think Nicky behaved as he did towards David Wilkerson?

room. They danced and smoked and drank. Suddenly there was a disturbance near the door. In walked David Wilkerson. He went across the room and offered his hand, saying, 'Nicky, I just wanted to shake hands with you and....'

Before he could finish, Nicky slapped him across the face – hard. Then he spat at him.

'They spat at Jesus too,' said David, 'and He prayed "Father,

Jesus Stuff

Nicky could not get the words out of his head, 'Jesus loves you'. Could it be that there was something in that Jesus stuff? Did someone really care about him? Nicky just did not know. In his confusion he did some crazy, savage things. He tried to kill his best friend with an ice-pick. He got hold of a pigeon and ripped the head from its body.

A week later David Wilkerson invited the Mau Mau gang to a meeting he was holding in a large hall. Nicky did not want to go.

'Hey, man,' one of his gang asked, 'you ain't chicken, are you?'

The angry reply came back: 'Nicky ain't afraid of no one – that skinny preacher, you, not even God.'

So the Mau Maus turned up for the meeting. Several gangs went. The noise was deafening. Nicky and his friends, dressed in their Mau Mau outfits, swaggered in. They walked up and down the aisles, tapping loudly with their sticks, shouting and whistling.

At one side a girl was playing an organ. All at once another girl walked out into the middle of the stage. She stood behind a microphone, waiting for the noise to stop. 'Hey, baby, wiggle it a bit,' someone shouted. 'How about a date, honey?' yelled another. The girl began to sing a religious song. As she sang, many gang members got up on their seats and began stamping, dancing and clapping. They were out to have fun.

The girl finished her song, almost in tears. She walked off the stage. David Wilkerson stepped forward. He talked for fifteen minutes. There were continual interruptions from youths shouting at him, knocking over chairs and threatening members of rival gangs.

Nicky did not hear much of what David was saying. He was remembering. His past actions flashed through his mind. He saw the parties and the girls, the stabbings and the sex, the drugs and the deaths, the hurt and the hatred. The more he remembered, the more guilty and ashamed he felt. He thought how rotten he was.

David Wilkerson came to the end of what he had to say. 'If you want your life changed, now is the time. Stand up! Those who want Jesus Christ to save them from their sins and be changed, stand up! Come forward!'

Nicky stood and went forward. So did over twenty other Mau Maus, as well as about thirty boys from other gangs.

What Do You Think?

1. Why do you think Nicky went to the religious meeting? What effect did it have on him? Why did Nicky want his life changed?

2. If Nicky had not gone to that meeting, but had still wanted to change his life, where do you think he could have gone for help?

A Changed Life

Nicky was a mixture of tears and laughter. He was happy, yet he was crying. He felt he was doing something right for a change. For the first time since he could remember, he prayed: 'Oh God, if You love me, come into my life. I'm tired of running. Come into my life and change me. Please change me.'

And something happened. All fear and hatred suddenly went. All the wrong and selfish thrills of a lifetime could not equal what he now felt – relief, freedom, happiness.

The next morning Nicky and the other Mau Maus who had decided to become Christians handed in their weapons at the local police station. They asked the policemen to autograph the Bibles that David Wilkerson had given them. At first the police thought this was a trick.

Nicky began to read the Bible. He found it was not so meaningless and dull as he had once thought. He started to go to church. He even went with David Wilkerson to one church to tell the people gathered there his story. While he was talking, something strange happened. As he spoke, his words became clearer and clearer. His voice became more and more normal. His throat was healed!

Once Nicky was shot at by

the Bishops as he came out of a church service. As he walked out of the door two cars across the street began to move. A woman screamed. He saw the gun barrels sticking out of the car windows. Shots were fired at him as the cars sped away. He ducked behind the door as the bullets smacked into the wall beside him.

Later he was knifed by a member of another gang. However, now he was a Christian he did not try to take revenge. He knew it was wrong to be violent.

Indeed he was so changed that after a while he decided to go to a Bible college and train to become a preacher.

Life at the Bible college was hard. The rules were strict. There was little spare time. And Nicky was not very clever. Sometimes he tried to make up for it by acting smart and showing off.

One morning Nicky and the rest of his class were standing while the teacher was saying a short prayer before the lesson began. In the middle of the prayer Nicky quietly moved the chair in front of him, that of a pretty girl called Gloria to whom he had taken rather a fancy.

When the teacher finished the prayer the class sat down on their chairs – all except Gloria, who fell back on the floor. She glared at Nicky. He laughed. As she swung her chair into place she jabbed the leg of the chair into Nicky's shin. It hurt him and he groaned. Everyone laughed.

This teasing started a friendship between Nicky and Gloria. Three years later they were married.

In the summer of 1960 Nicky went back to his former gang and talked to them about Jesus. He told them about the change in his life. As a result several Mau Maus became Christians and changed their way of life also.

Then Nicky went back to Puerto Rico to visit his family. Seeing the change in Nicky caused his mother and two of his brothers to become Christians too.

At the end of 1961 Nicky went to work at Teen Challenge Centre in Brooklyn, New York. Teen Challenge Centre was a home for boys and girls who needed special help. It was run by the preacher David Wilkerson. Here Nicky tried to help drug addicts and other young people who were in trouble.

One of the young people whom Nicky helped was Pedro. He was a strong, tall black lad. He was a Mau Mau. One day he had an argument in a bar with a youth who was a member of the Scorpion gang. He slashed him with a knife. The Scorpions promised revenge.

Nicky met Pedro in the street. He listened to his story and offered him a home at Teen Challenge Centre. Pedro willingly accepted. He stayed at the Centre for three

months. During that time he became a new person. He gave up the violence and wrong in his life and became a Christian.

Maria was a street-girl, a drug addict and a thief. She had been put in prison eleven times in the eight years since she had first taken drugs as a teenager. She stumbled into the Centre one evening. Her way of life changed too, through the help of Nicky and his wife. She went back to the streets to meet her former friends. She told them of God's love and forgiveness which she had found.

What Do You Think?

1. A change to a particular religious faith or lifestyle is sometimes called a 'conversion'. Nicky's conversion was a very emotional experience. What evidence in the story is there that it was not just a passing feeling?

2. Gang members and drug addicts who change their way of life often visit their former friends to tell them about their new religious faith or lifestyle. Why do you think they do this?

3. Why do some people think the Bible is dull?

Outreach for Youth

The young people who came to Teen Challenge Centre were usually older teenagers and those in their twenties. Those like Pedro and Maria were greatly helped. Yet there were many others who had lived an evil life so long that they could not easily give it up. They left the Centre no better than when they arrived. This made Nicky feel a failure. He thought it would be better if he worked among younger teenagers and children. These he could help in time.

So in August 1964 Nicky left Teen Challenge Centre. In the following year he set up his own 'Outreach for Youth' Home at Fresno, California. Many people gave him money to start his Home. It was a large building and the idea was that children and young teenagers could live there for a while, if their parents agreed.

On the first day Nicky walked around the streets looking for children in need of a home, he found Ruben. The boy was sitting in a doorway.

Nicky sat down beside him. 'What's your name?'

'What yer wanna know for?'

'Well you look kind of lonely and so I thought I'd talk to you.'

The boy looked at Nicky out of the corner of his eye and muttered 'Ruben'.

'How old are you, Ruben?' asked Nicky.

'Eleven.'

It turned out that Ruben was playing truant from school. His father was a drug addict, and he had no mother at home either.

'I've just opened a Home for kids like you,' said Nicky. 'Do you fancy coming to live in it?'

'You mean you *want* me to come?' Ruben sounded surprised.

'Sure,' went on Nicky, 'but we'll have to talk to your dad first.'

'Hell,' laughed Ruben, 'my old man'll be glad to get rid of me. The one you got to clear it with is my probation officer.'

The probation officer was delighted. That very same night Ruben went to live in the 'Outreach for Youth' Home.

Nicky found that many of the parents of the children wandering in the streets just did not care. Some were cruel to their children. Almost all the children and young teenagers were very unhappy, until they went to live in Nicky's Home.

One was a fifteen-year-old girl. Her rich parents were divorced. They did not bother about her. She was so sad that she tried to kill herself several times.

Today there are several Homes. One is in Puerto Rico itself. They are all run by Christians. They aim to give shelter and comfort to young people who feel unhappy or lonely or rejected. Several of those staying at any one time are already on probation or on drugs. The aim is to give them the love and warmth of family life which their own parents have not given them.

The helpers set the young people an example of how to live a helpful, honest and happy life. They teach them about Jesus as being someone who loves them. There is at least one Christian meeting every day, and the boys and girls are urged to pray each day on their own.

At the Homes there is always plenty to do. The helpers teach the young people many things, from how to understand the Bible to how to be good at basketball. Often in the evenings there are small groups learning some new game, hobby or interest.

Some of the young people are drug addicts when they arrive at the Homes. So there is usually someone on the staff who can help the young addicts to 'kick' the habit. Any young person who telephones, or calls in at the Home, will be helped if this is at all possible.

One boy who stayed at an 'Outreach for Youth' Home wrote this letter to Nicky:

My name is Carlos Miguel. I am fourteen years old. I began taking drugs and drinking alcohol when I was twelve years old. I did not attend school and I did not respect my parents. My parents had to send me to a juvenile court to see if the court could help me. But appearing in court and the threats of the magistrate did not make any difference. The advice of my social workers did not change me either. Everything seemed in vain. I was on my way to drug addiction, jail and death.

One day my social worker spoke to me about Outreach for Youth. I thought it was a place like the ones I knew. But when I arrived I discovered that it was quite different from what I had thought. It was a Christian home ... it was a home full of love ... a home where God was.

I have been at the Home for the past seven months. They have been the happiest seven months of my life. I thank God for Outreach for Youth and for the people who have helped us. They have stopped me from becoming one more addict. When I came I could not read or write properly, but here I was taught. Now I am attending school.

In 1978 Nicky visited Britain for the first time. He spoke to hundreds of young people in Leeds, Newcastle, Leicester and Birmingham. His message to them was simple: 'Give Jesus Christ a chance just like I did. I know He will change your whole life.'

In 1994 Nicky set up TRUCE to help inner-city youngsters escape from gang life, drug addiction and a life of crime. 'TRUCE' stands for 'To Reach Urban Children Everywhere'.

Says Nicky, 'These kids are hardened criminals. They don't respond to parents, teachers or prison. We offer them the choice of feeling secure other than by being a member of a gang. You can't go to gang members and talk about hell. They know what hell is about. They live in hell. We need to let them know about heaven.'

In 1998 Nicky launched a national Pray for Teen America day. 'I want children to experience the same love and compassion from God that saved my life,' he explains.

'I am content with life, and happy,' Nicky told a newspaper reporter in 1978. 'I buried Nicky Cruz nineteen years ago and he is dead. Now I am alive in Christ.'

Today Nicky feels it is important that he is famous not just for being a former gang leader. 'I'm famous because Jesus Christ loves me and I love Him,' he says. 'I was full of bitterness and evil. I hated God. I hated people. Most of all, I hated myself. Then I became a completely new creature through God's Holy Spirit.'

What Do You Think?

1. Why do some children truant from school? How can they be encouraged to go to school?

2. Why are some adults cruel to children in their care?

3. How can being unable to read or write properly affect a person's life?

4. 'Teenagers won't listen to people in authority who have let them down all their lives,' says Nicky. What sort of people in authority do you think he means? How may they have let down teenagers?

Although he belongs to their grandparents' generation, Nicky still captures the attention of teenagers today. 'It's amazing to see 10 000 young people packed into a large hall to hear Nicky speak,' says one inner-city church minister.

'All I knew was this guy was an O.G. [original gangster],' explains one gang member, 'and he was 'aving this big meeting tonight.'

'Teenagers won't listen to people in authority who have let them down all their lives,' says Nicky. 'But they will respond to a message about God if it comes from others who have survived the same living hell.'

Nicky spends much of his time travelling around the U.S.A. and visiting other countries, speaking about his work and the problems of the young people.

Biographical Notes

1938	Nicky Cruz was born 6 December near the village of Las Piedras on the island of Puerto Rico.
1955	He went to New York, and joined the Mau Mau gang when he was sixteen.
1958	He became a Christian.
1958–61	He attended the Latin American Bible Institute at La Puente, California.
1961	He married Gloria, a student at the Institute. (They now have four daughters.)
1962–65	He and his wife worked at the Teen Challenge Centre in Brooklyn, New York.
1965	Nicky started his 'Outreach for Youth' movement in Fresno, California. In 1974 this became Nicky Cruz Outreach and is now based in Colorado Springs.
1968	Nicky's first book, *Run Baby Run*, was published. It has sold over 12 million copies in the U.S.A. and has been printed in 43 languages.
1974–92	Nicky made about thirty tours of Britain and Ireland to speak about his conversion to the Christian faith.

Today Nicky Cruz is an Assemblies of God (Pentecostal) church minister.

Note The story of David Wilkerson is told in more detail in *Friend of Drug Addicts,* by R. J. Owen, in the original Faith in Action series or *In His Service. Book 2,* both published by RMEP.

Things To Do

1 Create a cartoon strip showing the most important events in the story of Nicky Cruz.

2 Produce a map of North America including the United States of America and the West Indies.

(a) Mark on the map the states of California and Pennsylvania, the cities of New York, Fresno and Colorado Springs, and the island of Puerto Rico.

(b) Alongside the name of each place, write a short sentence explaining its connection with Nicky Cruz.

(c) Explain why the people of Puerto Rico speak Spanish and how the island became part of the U.S.A.

3 (a) Make two displays out of newspaper and magazine cuttings: one showing the good things young people do and the other showing the trouble they may get into.

(b) Was there more material available for one display than the other? Discuss your findings and whether your displays give a fair impression of young people.

4 Write a prayer which might be used by those thinking about young people who are suffering from drug addiction **or** an unhappy home life **or** living on the streets.

5 Produce a report about the work of an organization which tries to help children and teenagers, such as the Children's Society, ChildLine, NSPCC or NCH. Use an Internet search engine or relevant Web-site to obtain up-to-date information on their work.

6 Write a poem to show how you feel about **either** cruelty to animals **or** cruelty to children.

7 Design a poster with a suitable slogan and picture to advertise **either** one of Nicky Cruz's TRUCE meetings **or** Pray for Teen America day (see page 18).

8 Improvise a short dramatic sketch based on **one** of the following parts of the story of Nicky Cruz:

(a) Nicky's home life (page 4)
Characters: Nicky, Nicky's mother, Nicky's father, Nicky's brothers and sister, some visiting spiritualists

(b) Confrontation with a gang (pages 5–6)
Characters: Nicky, several members of the gang called the Bishops

(c) Confrontation with David Wilkerson (pages 10–11)
Characters: Nicky, David, trumpet-player, onlookers, Nicky's friends

9 Find a copy of the words of 'Onward! Christian Soldiers', the hymn which Nicky heard being played on the trumpet. Try to listen to the tune.

(a) Find out all you can about the person who wrote the words of that hymn.

(b) Suggest reasons why the hymn is not as popular amongst Christians as it used to be (clue: language and imagery).

(c) Listen to the music of some modern Christian song-writers and singers, such as Amy Grant, Matt Redman, Noel Richards and Darlene Zschech. Why might such music appeal more to young people than more traditional hymns?

10 Prepare a mime or creative dance showing **either** what happened at the meeting in the large hall (page 12) **or** the experiences of Carlos Miguel (page 18).

11 Imagine you are a preacher. Prepare a two-minute talk which could be used at a street-corner to persuade passers-by to think about God.

12 Read a story of a well-known person whose life has been influenced by God – such as TV entertainers Tommy Cannon and Bobby Ball, soccer player Gavin Peacock and athlete Jonathan Edwards. Present the story in an imaginative way.

Questions for Assessment or Examination Candidates

13 Nicky Cruz says that inner-city youngsters 'need to ... know about heaven' (page 18).

(a) What do Christians believe about heaven, hell, purgatory and eternal life? (4 marks)

(b) What is the difference between resurrection and reincarnation? (6 marks)

(c) What different evidence is there for life after death? (You may wish to consider communications from the dead received at spiritualist meetings, near-death experiences, visions of angels, and so on.) (5 marks)

(d) How may belief in an afterlife give meaning and purpose to a person's life and affect a person's attitudes and behaviour? (5 marks)

14 Answer the following structured question:

(a) Describe different ways in which people claim to experience God. (5 marks)

(b) Some people claim to know what God is like because they believe they have experienced God. How else might religious believers know what God is like? (5 marks)

(c) Explain why other people believe that all religious experiences are imagined and not real. (5 marks)

(d) 'Religious experiences are all as valid as each other.' Do you agree? Give reasons for your opinion, showing that you have thought about more than one point of view. (5 marks)

Religious and Moral Education Press
*A division of SCM–Canterbury Press Ltd,
a wholly owned subsidiary of
Hymns Ancient & Modern Ltd
St Mary's Works, St Mary's Plain
Norwich, Norfolk NR3 3BH*

Copyright © 1980, 2000 R. J. Owen

R. J. Owen has asserted his right under
the Copyright, Designs and Patents Act,
1988, to be identified as Author of this
Work.

*All rights reserved. No part of this
publication may be reproduced, stored in
a retrieval system, or transmitted, in any
form or by any means, electronic,
electrostatic, magnetic tape, mechanical,
photocopying, recording or otherwise,
without permission in writing from the
publishers.*

First published 1980 under the title: *The
Killer Who Cried*

First reprinted under present title 1982

New edition first published 2000

ISBN 1 85175 194 7

Designed and typeset by
TOPICS – The Creative Partnership,
Exeter

Cover illustration by Jane Taylor

Printed in Great Britain by
Brightsea Press, Exeter for
SCM–Canterbury Press Ltd, Norwich

Notes for Teachers

The first Faith in Action books were published in the late 1970s and the series has remained popular with both teachers and pupils. However, much in education has changed over the last twenty years, such as the development of both new examination syllabuses in Religious Studies and local agreed syllabuses for Religious Education which place more emphasis on pupils' own understanding, interpretation and evaluation of religious belief and practice, rather than a simple knowledge of events. This has encouraged us to amend the style of the Faith in Action Series to make it more suitable for today's classroom.

The aim is, as before, to tell the stories of people who have lived and acted according to their faith, but we have included alongside the main story questions which will encourage pupils to think about the reasons for the behaviour of our main characters and to empathize with the situations in which they found themselves. We hope that pupils will also be able to relate some of the issues in the stories to other issues in modern society, either in their own area or on a global scale.

The 'What Do You Think?' questions may be used for group or class discussion or for short written exercises. The 'Things to Do' at the end of the story include ideas for longer activities and more-structured questions suitable for assessment or examination practice.

In line with current syllabus requirements, as Britain is a multifaith society, Faith in Action characters will be selected from a wide variety of faith backgrounds and many of the questions may be answered from the perspective of more than one faith.

CMB, 1997

Acknowledgements
The publishers would like to thank the original General Editors of the Faith in Action Series, Geoffrey Hanks and David Wallington, for their contribution to the development of the first edition of this book.